Talisman

Talisman

poems by

Lisa C. Krueger

RED HEN PRESS | *Pasadena, CA*

Book design and layout by Natasha Castro

Cover design by Nicholas Smith

Library of Congress Cataloging-in-Publication Data

Krueger, Lisa C.

[Poems. Selections]

Talisman / Lisa C. Krueger.—First edition.

pages cm

ISBN: 978-1-59709-545-7 (tradepaper)

ISBN: 978-1-59709-271-5 (casebound)

I. Title.

PS3611.R84A6 2014

811'.6—dc23

2013039409

The Los Angeles County Arts Commission, the National Endowment for the Arts, the Pasadena Arts & Cultural Commission and the City of Pasadena Cultural Affairs Division, the Los Angeles Department of Cultural Affairs, the Dwight Stuart Youth Fund, and Sony Pictures Entertainment partially support Red Hen Press.

First Edition

Published by Red Hen Press

www.redhen.org

Acknowledgments

Grateful acknowledgment is made to the editors of the following publications in which these poems appeared:

Arroyo Literary Review, "Saturdays Across the Border"; *Atlanta Review,* "There Is No Echo"; *The Cape Rock,* "Why We Don't Skype"; *damselfly press,* "Earth Before Blooms"; *Glass: A Journal of Poetry,* "Secured Cushions, Beer and Olives"; *Naugatuck River Review,* "What She Felt"; *Oberon,* "Talisman"; and *Prairie Schooner,* "Drought As Desire," "Peach Jam," "Release."

"There Is No Echo" also was featured in *Hometown Pasadena* and received an International Poetry Prize from *Atlanta Review.*

I would like to thank Tracy K. Smith, Jim Moore, April Bernard, Mark Wunderlich, Brenda Shaughnessy, Ed Ochester, Sven Birkerts, Victoria Clausi, Kate Gale and Mark Cull. Thank you to my friends and family, all beloved.

for Bob

Contents

I

II

III

We'll dream of a longer summer
but this is the one we have:
—Adrienne Rich

Talisman

I

What She Felt

In L.A. my sister's car wrapped like foil
around a pole as the sun sank,

offering illusions of a softened world,
the other car careening, reversing,

screeching off into the almost dark.
Bystanders listened for sirens, watched

the medics' *Jaws of Life* pull metal
from mangled limbs that convulsed.

They lay her on pavement,
forced rods into her skull.

They called what they did a *halo.*
They said she couldn't feel the metal

clasp her flesh, burrow into her bones.
They said she couldn't feel

the breath machine, or the one
that cleaned her blood.

What she felt, they said,
wasn't what we felt.

My sister surfed every sunset.
Her hair was wet.

Underpass

I swaddled you in the early years,
our mother calling out *Be careful,*
she needs to breathe.

Began to lie when you asked me
if I was afraid of the dark.
Couldn't stop.

Wanted to believe in light, in sweeping
floors, folding clothes, placing what belongs
in a drawer. Closing drawers.

The day you left
you wore my cast-offs.
They never fit.

I want to tell you I am
the homesick one. Driving
by your underpass, imagining

you love the night, its asphalt spangling,
its traffic rushing small waves
against the concrete vault.

Girl, I'll House You

—Jungle Brothers

I

I set my house on fire
my sister says, taking a match
to small possessions, the photos,

the certificate of graduation
after the car accident,
whispering into her room phone

House me, Sister.
Through my Victorian window
I watch a late winter storm,

bare trees flailing:
I am burning,
burning it down

says this sister,
my only sister, my
best kept secret,

disabled sect of self.
Sister! Stop! I cry,
hearing the lick of flame:

she is sick
of facility love, all day long
between two demented men

hand in hand in hand,
sick
of the mechanical bed

all night long.
She wants to burn everything,
she would rather *die wild*

in a street's asphalt rut
than a house like this—
House me—

at the next place nurses
keep her cigs, she has to ask
for a light.

II

my best kept secret

this damage, this

disabled sect of self

diminished, braving

fate, the winds

rage, bare trees

refuse to break

power out, can't

log on

watching branches

flail against sky

we burnished

climbed limestone

if we fell, we would

slide into the sea

the music of beach

wind in wild sage

cries of foxes and gulls

My Locked Unit Routine

I am ringing the visitor bell waiting
for someone to buzz me in,

holding my gift-pack of cigarettes,
my careful words. I am walking past the wall

that buckles, its chinks thick with Kleenex,
to the fluorescent ward, the world

of common rooms and plastic chairs
bolted to the floor. My sister discerned

that *The Outside* called her names,
spit on her, dragged her across dirt,

left her for dead. *She doesn't*
want to see you, the nurse says,

she is very angry today. I am searching
the faces as though she is here,

knowing she is wrapped in her stained parka,
lying on her bed. Down the hall

I hear her shout that this is not the day
she asked for, this is not the sister.

Intrepid

We like the tea garden at
the psych ward where
moon spreads its veil on
a patch of grass. We sit up
straight on curvy benches
otherwise you slide off.
A girl named Vanessa walks
around the edge 1,000 times,
close to the bars, clanging out
a rhyme. No one visits
Vanessa, my sister says.
Vanessa is all bones. Meds
bloated my sister's body.
She wears her parka zipped,
Vanessa wears a sleeveless shirt.
Light from the unit bounces
off scars. For years my sister
and I liked to drink tea
at Descanso beneath giant
camellias while we watched
carp in the stream. Shadows
and cool yet never cold.
We study nurses behind glass.
Each time Vanessa passes
she chimes *Hello, Love!*
My sister's body aches
from weight *but I never*
wanted to be small.

Delusions Are Hardest to Treat

My sister and I were raised
on christmas slogans

some things have to be believed
to be seen

yet no one ever showed
to grant our wish

grinning at me
beneath the gash

of a santa hat
my sister confides

mrs claus was a nurse
her delusion is

she's a helper
how are we

here again
with our stubborn faith?

newly committed
patients can't wear

laces clasps straps anything
that binds or scrapes

no bras allowed
everything slips or flops

mrs claus nestles
on the tv bench

cradling the remote
like a baby

Broken Tail

At the Labyrinth party we walk woodchip paths
that spiral in nautilus design
while trying to be "mindful," as instructed,
since our hosts are believers,

claiming the universe listens to people
who wander in circles
then offers a response.
Most of us carry drinks from the bar.

My sister reaches the center by leaning on her cane
then drags it behind her on the way out
like our childhood cat carried her broken tail,
emboldened by its useless weight.

The party stacks up behind us
like traffic on the 110,
a curve of humanity waiting,
no one honking or trying to pass.

She is pausing ahead of me, turning back
as though to share some secret,
a school girl confiding answers,
certain of truth.

Pre-measured

This home leave, my sister

wants to bake a pumpkin pie.

Sometimes she forgets to eat

or when she eats she forgets

to chew and swallow

before the next bite.

The soap turning around and

round in her hands:

I have reminded her that baking

requires cleanliness, that

our creations should be

pure, free of germs.

How pure is this? she says,

holding her hands above her head.

Prodigal

I was mourning. Then the deer
who ate flowers, mangled fences,
began to swim in our pool. Each night

I crossed the lawn to watch her,
the weighted strokes moving water in waves.
I envied how she inhabited beauty,

didn't need to cultivate it, practice its deceit.
For weeks she floated and paddled,
buoyant against any depth.

I no longer feared she would drown.
I began to talk, not knowing if she heard.
Once I called her Mother.

She swam to me, animal face dispassionate,
fierce, a glint of silvery down
echoing the flash of my heart.

You are old I said to her.
I listened to the patterns of her breath,
the animal vowels, the voice.

Ladies' Night

She waits until the second drink
to tell them about the affair.
Or the third, so much Chardonnay
slipping away. They stand at the island
eating baby carrots.

She read that machines transform larger ones
before they turn old and bitter, spin
and shave them into bullets. Her turn
to cook, how to tell them there is only soup?
She can't remember hunger for food.

She wants to talk about the affair,
how unexpected it was yet somehow
fated, the way her husband
recoils from touch even in sleep,
both of them startling if one should roll over.

The women are peering at each other,
comparing nasolabial folds.
Whose are deep, who wants to try filler.
Will it hurt? They have heard that weight
more than age makes them worse.

When she begins the women are holding
their cheeks, tips of fingers at the top of bone.
Each is lifting her skin up high, just to see.

Swap Years

They remember fabled days
with fondness as though they'd do it
again, leave babies with sitters,
take turns with houses,

drink a little before they walk in:
no one looks straight at anyone,
no one's tempted to say
what are you doing here

in the abyss of fast drunk sex
decreed by random keys
from the party bowl
that offer momentary magic.

How they remade themselves,
rewinding time to New Year's,
or homecoming, or the honeymoon
they never had; the sleeping children,

the sitter who watched the clock
frozen forever, unless they said so,
unless they claimed the crush of years,
the desolation, as their own.

Opening the Mouth

They were pioneers *extraordinaire,* brave
to leave small towns upstate or mid-west
for the unknown, *California* not a place
but a foreign tongue to *Batavia, Emporia.*

They yearned to speak the mystery
in rented bungalows above *Windansea,*
gathering for drinks, parties that never stopped,
meeting at the famous studio party,

my mother posing, my father grabbing
the artist's brush to blacken her portrait's eyes.
The vocabulary was liquid—flat champagne
in bed the morning after, then scotch.

Other women did this, too, watched a husband
sleep in his suit: my mother's tongue swelled
against a chipped tooth or a festered lip.
She learned to smile without opening her mouth.

The day he slipped away she watched him
turn his face toward her, his words insistent,
garbled, the nurse declaring afterward
he must have had something to say.

The Broken

My brother reaching through spindles
for golden light, the bannister breaking,

the chandelier that clipped his fall
swaying, cracking. Toddler body

motionless; mother in the corner.
Shattered teeth.

On Valentine's, the cake's sugar heart
burst when we stabbed it with forks.

We splintered the bony limbs of our lemon
tree. Climbed it, bit into bitter rinds,

sucked juice to see who puckered more.
Children! Time to come in. Come in:

they took us to a bomb shelter
behind the house, a hideout

we'd never noticed. Doors opening
to darkness, our vision adjusting

to rubbled stairs, we stumbled
onto edges of concrete ruins.

This is where you go in war, they said.
Wait for the all-clear.

The Summer of Fish

That storm summer our father
taught us how to slide a short knife
under flesh, sever the unnecessary.

Razored edges of slick bodies
nicked our fingers,
scales stuck to our thighs.

We washed away blood
with hoses, our palms
stinging. Sometimes my hands

felt a flash of gold burning
into me. I couldn't
bear the stupidity of fish.

I learned to steer a boat,
to cast a line for what
I never wanted.

No one noticed
what anyone caught,
no one cared

about who slipped out
of their skin,
who swam away.

Saturdays Across the Border

Everything a bargain, a concession.
Grabbing the hand of her sister's guy
hard, wanting to hurt, walking
through smells of burning rubber
and carnitas, breathing in the hot oil.
They watched her parents
fight about cheap leather furniture
that would fill the house,
horse and cow hides barely dry,
thick with odor of animal.
She coveted the sudden unimportance
of tears, how her little sister looked away
from what was meant to be hers.
The boyfriend's hand gripping back
so she felt pain, neither letting go.
The father bargaining in mock Spanish.
She decided to hoard everything
until she couldn't feel,
caressing his wide palm, laughing
at his hate, walking behind the others
to jai-alai where men would slam
their beauty against walls.

Safety

Sometimes my brother sounded heroic
behind his door, the still soprano voice
straining at Superman's theme song

while he ran in circles of small leaps,
air whooshing around a towel cape.
We kept our doors closed for Dad,

his voice against walls at all hours
in the sales pitch or the night rage
when Mom's words threaded the dark,

stitching together what came apart.
I learned not to listen, to imagine
the island of white linens.

Sometimes I peeked at my brother
when he crouched on his ledge,
the cape snug with a safety pin.

Once I found him on the grass,
lying against the cape, not moving.
Did you jump, I asked, standing over him.

I am going to tell on you, I said, knowing
I never would. His safety pin undone,
the steel prick against his neck.

The Fighting Ceases

The car is in trouble so we stop
at the only light the Mojave offers, a

small civilization, mechanic, snack shop,
motel, zoo. *We are lucky we made it*

our parents repeat, *lucky, lucky*
to us kids in back who have watched the night

for hours, how it goes on and on,
never halting, its resonance quieting

the voices up front, the whole ride
a motion of dream

before the irregular beat of what
came loose. *Could be a day,*

could be a week the mechanic says.
We kids keep moving.

We walk through a shack with mesh cages,
two monkeys, a cat, a snake:

outside our parents are holding hands.
Each time I exit

I study their profile,
hoping luck will hold.

Bank Teller

My grandmother stood for thirty years
behind short metal bars, resting her hands

on a small slab of marble meant for cash.
When she died we learned she had bled

for months, pleaded with doctors for a diagnosis,
something she could say was hers.

My mother raised us far from her own small town.
Nights, I heard her cry.

The inheritance bought a marble moon,
a coffee table that beamed indulgence:

we leaned against marble
for drinks on crystal coasters.

I wondered if we were rich enough to replace
the frayed afghans and battered bookshelves.

Dad spittled his drunk laugh
when he fell on the table.

We used our hands to pick up shards
that slivered skin.

We kids laughed, shielding our eyes
from slices of moon glinting in darkness.

Guest Farm Pardon

She touched the flank of a boar
lying in the sun, eyes closed, dirt
encrusted in stubby tusks.
She grazed the stiffness of his bristle,
the soft languor of animal serenity.
Her hands stroked quickly,
tenderly, a flash of light.
The boar did not move.
Most nights she yearns for sleep
but feels afraid, as though
she must fix her life.
If she thinks about the boar,
she can let go. She imagines
him awake, walking his pen,
assuming the possibilities of night.
She imagines salvation,
its moisture of hay, of fetid skin,
the vigilant carnal scent.

Allotment

My mother hides chocolate from herself,
discovering it at the back of the cupboard
after she washes dinner dishes.

My father drinks scotch in the den,
I am supposed to be upstairs.
She doesn't know I stand at the door

watch her reach her treat,
snap off a single chunk, her mouth open.
We kids never touch her stash.

Their fights are growing worse.
Even across the house I hear echoes.
Sometimes when she puts chocolate

on her tongue, my mother's body shivers;
I never shiver when I eat chocolate,
even if I hide it. Hiding:

I want to step forward, I want to speak.
I wait until she is dead,
until I am the woman at the kitchen sink,

my husband's arms closing around me,
shivering, saying to myself,
Want more! Want more!

II

Voracious at Café Literati, Santa Monica

The other women refuse bread,
argue over which country
is more spiritual, India or Bali.
She listens like a foreigner.
Birds at their feet search for crumbs,
she feels a small softness
brush her calf. The women
look elegant, sleek as horses,
staying on course. They stab
at salads, claim no appetite.
She is skinny, excoriated by grief,
every fiber of being gaunt,
starving. Yet her heart's
weight: she feels fat
sitting near them. Picking
at her roll, dropping fragments
at her feet. Longing to devour
cake at the counter, glory
in the waste of the world.

Condolence Note at the Kitchen Table

She notices the odor of ripeness from bananas,
wondering why some people need to be kind,

as though genetically required, always
remembering the compliment, the best

babysitter's phone number.
She used to make banana bread, never

wanting to waste something good.
Sorry; sad: Every word has happened before,

every sympathy expressed. She puts her
pen down. If she baked today, no one

would eat her bread. Everyone is on a *diet*.
Die with a *t*. She saved all the condolences

about her mother. She wants to write down
the revolution of birth after someone dies,

the fierceness she could claim,
but people don't do that.

Resistance

Our rental skidded
then righted itself, the deer

cinematic, obstreperous
with breath and force.

The highway had been silent
for so long, just endless

black road, the flank of bare trees.
Then the animal, unexpected,

even though we had passed signs.
We were out of state, out

of place, wanted to believe
in leaving without maps,

without reservations, agreeing
we would find what we needed.

Do not hit her I begged, knowing
a car can only slow so much.

Some things are irrefutable,
the hand on my leg,

the darkness between us
that didn't matter.

Cross Country

When he left it was dark
though birdsong sporadically
lisped outside the window,

the here and there of sound,
the way wakening
comes in increments.

Good-bye, he whispered,
not touching me, just words
to hold in sleep.

My loneliness was an ocean:
every word that set sail
capsized.

I saved myself with symbols.
Emptiness became my sojourn,
my necessary travel.

I dreamt until it was real, this way
of being with him, the land
a blanket spread between us.

Theft

After years of seasons
their summers grew simple:

they learned to laugh
at a peach's slick stickiness,

the languorous evenings
when darkness did not come.

Yet August had gone missing;
only heat parched their yearning

for the yellow month
with its sea of desire.

They foraged summer berries tongued
with sweet, infused their sleep

with scents of pleasured earth
that rose from the darkened lawn.

They stepped away from themselves;
night blooms masked theft.

Someone Might See

We drank from a spring's
open sky, its thickness awakening
new thirst. Dense tissues
sustained our weight,
leaf-sweet layers
cushioned our brash reach,
one person touching another
for restoration, for inheritance
of desire that progressed
in waves of light
through trees, the world
opening its arms.
Get dressed, fire in the sky,
in the spring of water,
all elements undisguised.
We found our clothes then,
went on with our lives.

Pleasure in Darkness

What I sleep against.
I rise with first birds to watch
light magnify the San Gabriels.

We never will see this together:
so much of our lives felt alone.
Don't deny it. Don't deny me this.

Mist in the valley, blue mist, as you rest.
How can a sun be magnificent one moment,
ordinary the next? When you sleep

I still feel you near: I dream of you
in waking words, while you dream of me
in slumber; in this way we are together.

The coppery bones of the valley gleam.
We make love to our past. Lately when
I touch you, I feel history in your skin.

Drought As Desire

My daughter got ill the year
they tore out eucalyptus

along the 101, roots
suspended in air, no more

orange groves to protect
in a land of mini-malls

I stumbled along my own blockades
believing friends would come

with food in baskets thinking
there were barriers against blackness

when seasons stopped I accepted
drought as though it were life

breathed the scorch of it
(no dinners left by the back door)

while rumors whirled
that some were healed by water

we had no water we learned
to harvest in thirst

The Old Story Follows Us

I feel reassured
the hills are still green
even though brown brush
shows through like beard scruff.
I want to run my hand
across the ridge.
The hay wagon jostles
friendly strangers, our
shoulders, legs touch.
Already hay is in my boots.
My daughter leans
against me, pretending
the wagon has done this,
forced an intimacy
between two people
desperate to grow apart.

Peach Jam

We use our fingers to slide skin
off late summer peaches, separate
flesh from pit. Our hands glisten
with juice when we stir the jam.

Afterwards we rest on the hammock,
watching sky. We don't talk about
the give-away boxes in the garage
or the ticket my daughter has bought.

Our lopsided position disturbs
our cocoon, which shivers and tilts.
So we adjust, move muscles
to realign our bodies.

Sometimes I can't feel
my arms or legs, as though
my mind, with its hollows
of thought, isolates.

Today, my child resting
against me, I think of a tree
without fruit, how emptiness
allows branches to move.

She drapes a leg over the side,
pushes off against the ground
and we swing, shin to shin,
sky above, just rocking.

Why We Don't Skype

Maybe my daughter moves away
so I can't watch the illness

how she beds it
like an old love

comfortable in the half-dream of it
the compromise
(chronic, inflamed)

on the phone her high wire voice,
it's just an episode, don't, please don't

I have not said *let me fly out*
let me call the doctor
let me cry

hearing the circling hawk
of my heart
she hangs up

friends say *let her go*
as though I have been holding on

I was not holding on
to anything but hope

I want to rage
about the loss

yet no one loves
the flailing woman
at the sideline

friends say *look, in a way*
she is blossoming

let her bloom as though
I forgot the rules

my daughter has bloomed
since birth,

I am the one folding in,
petal after petal

History of Clothes

The young mothers in yoga pants
disrupt some sense of what
people used to call *decorum*
as though nothing merits dressing up
beyond the supple body.
Their eyes shimmer through her.
She tries to imagine feeling young again
and *minimalist* like this but can't.
She remembers a primal weight of days,
the astonishment of limitations.
Everything she did she dreamed.
Never got it right. Someone was dirty,
needing a bath or fresh shirt.
Someone was running away.
Or returning, always wanting.
At a distance the complexity,
the layer upon layer of choices
that wove a life, even the threads
of lost opportunity, stun.

Opening to Light

He closed his eyes against brilliance
then blew, laughing as each candle succumbed.
Exactly like years gathered in his mind,
gleaming with the brevity of flame.

He claimed simple desires,
another season for birds to nest
with the skein of a misplaced sweater,
more afternoons at the café

where his waitress wore rainbows
on her wrist. Light from this cake
felt harsh, a domestic blaze of accusation:
personal flaws floated like ashes

in the wick smoke. He had wished
that his wife would abandon him,
that she would stop waiting
for the man he had vowed to become.

Yet she held him each night.
Year after year they closed
windows and doors;
he wanted insurrection.

He wanted to open everything,
he wanted to rip off the roof.
Wildness would offer shelter.
That would be heaven.

Private Lessons

The dog trainer says I need more instruction—
I am not in command. I swear
I have proven myself: I yank my puppy
if he walks ahead too far.

Look, the trainer says, *who is the leader?*
He jumps on you. He barks at other dogs.
More lessons, more money, more time.
The trainer says he should know.

He trained famous dogs, the Rin Tin Tins
and Lassies. *Man's best friend,* he chuckles.
This pup is on the fast track to Best Friend.
He notices, lets me talk as long as I want.

His hours are flexible. He keeps it
light. I don't want to make him sit,
or lie down, or heel, I just want him
to stay interested.

The trainer certifies that I can make my dog
stay for good. I can walk away.
He will obey my rules.
He will wait for me.

Dependence

I shine a hard light. Then we may touch.
Dirt and seeds. Comet-like.

My version of unfiltered sun.
You think I jest? I am serious.

I will tie you up. I will search every crevice
for what scares me:

isolation. Aren't you bone?
Not quite blood of my blood, or flesh,

but numinous. Vertebraic.
I have watched death do nothing

but rotate the axis.
Most of us still spin, undiscovered.

Here is my final question,
leveled at the bull's-eye of what you call

heart: Sheath of the innocent core?
You to me? Fire to fire, our fingers

touch tips in a jet above the Midwest
but all you see is land. Look here!

Enclosed

The window's dangled
strand of fake sea glass

shatters ocean
across room,

through pane
a drought glares

bleak racks
a parking lot's

rivering heat.
Some things seem

fixed in truth:
the passage of time;

enclosures of days
when longing

swells in light.
Glass

knows how
to survive:

crushed,
tumbled,

reconstituted:
a blue world

I harbor
for you.

III

Once I Loved a Marine

Summer after summer we searched
for bisque tokens of good fortune,
even the chipped ones with broken
flowers, collecting them in buckets
or cups of our hands; if I found one
I called out Sand dollar! and my father
replied Sand dollar! My father only talked
when we wandered, he told me
that growing up in Kansas
he never saw the sea, once
he snuck onto a golf course
almost drowned in the pond.
Sometimes I hid them in pockets
until they crumbled. The year my father
drank himself back to Okinawa,

I walked alone, preserving in my mind

our tokens of conversation, what

we used to say, or might have said.

I called out to the water,

impervious to its vast reply.

Earth Before Blooms

One boy lisped his declarations
so I couldn't grasp the slips of sound,
Try again I said, watching his mouth.

You love me, he said. We sat behind
a trellis of sweet peas, touching,
comparing skin, his pale against mine.

Every afternoon I ran from my barren yard
to the patchwork of his mother's garden,
its fragrance inflamed by late heat.

I loved the way she carried a watering can
to dry spots or knelt among plants
to tend the troughs of seeds.

Love me, he said, when we sat on the bench,
tangling and leaning against each other,
the light swirling.

I closed my eyes, imagined the earth
before blooms, the grit, the damp, the dark
remorseless song of it, and I did.

The Bargain

The night my husband gave me
a diamond necklace
I locked myself in the bathroom
and rocked,
fists beating against thighs,
nails scratching skin

in deep striations, his voice
Unlock the door, soft at first,
imploring, then louder, scared,
angry. Rocking against darkness
that gagged me, bound me,
under the door the snake of stars.

My mother had just died,
I was bereft beyond anything
I thought possible, a shell,
symbol of someone called wife,
called friend, absent, floating
in a dream dusk.

I knew what he wanted,
he wanted me to touch him
like I used to, open
to that crescendo of light
that belonged to us.
He wanted me to *let him in,*

let him claim the space my mother had filled,
her luminosity outshining him for years.
I opened to the yearning that sorrow begets,
how we reach for another to remake our loss,
skin to skin richness that never lasts,
the only wealth I needed to live.

Because Pam Pulled Weeds After Chemo

Sparse sunflowers bend
from late birth near vines
of beans that twist
their knots of death.
I kneel in flowered fennel
and weeds
to offer my mistakes,
the rules, the careful design.
This garden glitters
in wanton seeds
that yearn for a turn,
a go, a chance to touch
the stippled, the dappled,
every poet's asylum
of dirt and stem.
What dies remains
in staggered stalks,
corn skeletons sheltering
seedlings of lettuce.
Anguish, too, lifts,
circles outward,
circles back, opening
the gate in myself
to the fallow field.

Last Encore (Concerto Delle Donne)

She said you know I need to go to Santa Fe,
the opera, you know

(the tenor's broad branches)

I said if you need to

She said opera and you know the gardens

(tangle of staccato against legato)

behind walls even though I have no more
platelets or whites

(the pause, the half-note)

I said maybe you shouldn't go

She said I need to go I need to
hear the orchestra one last time

(bel canto of coralbells)

even though I see now why some give up
since no energy is utter silence

(heuchera of song)

I said remember the energy from plants

(accompagnato of body)

She said sometimes I dream
the sounds of flowers

(tessitura of tulips)

She said you know
I am learning to sing

(splendored cadenza)

(aria of green)

Release

My mother laboring, whispering
Your hands look old! End of summer,

jasmine in the air. Smell of season's end.
My gardener's hands have deepened

in dark splotches, gnarled from digging,
yielding to bright land.

My daughter walking as woman, wide hips,
slender neck, the turn in her shoulders,

pain's chronicity confining her frame,
bars of bones that burn.

My mother dying, saying *This*
is harder for you than for me.

My head on her lap. My daughter's hand
on mine. Sometimes morning is hard.

My daughter says she struggles to get going,
but once she is up, she can make it.

Picnic With Separate Cars

Abundance transcribed as river, as table,
a family, place of reunion, heart
of the matter. Our grown children
drive in separate cars, unpack
disparate picnics. So glad
to see each other, to savor
our bites of bread, sips of wine.

One of my sons says *Maybe next year*
there will be another of us! His wife
looks away, watches the river
that sings to us, growing louder.
She sits in my mother's spot,
holding herself as my mother did,
arms crossed, *self-contained,*

her whole body leaning
toward my son. The wine's
afternoon light rivers a world,
a thin place where time flows
both ways. Afterimage shimmers
flecks of eye and lip: when faces blur
I pretend everyone is here.

When We Took Our Time

Yesterday I saw a couple kiss
outside the market, long,
slow, maybe with tongue,

their bodies almost still
as though movement
might disturb the universe.

People stopped pushing carts
to stare, some arms
heavy with groceries.

They were very old
yet his hands
caressed her face

like you caressed mine
that first morning
we bought bread and fruit,

walked out of the market,
the bloom of chrome and tires
a field of stars.

Anywhere

I want to tell you I walked today
fantasizing about new love,
the man was you but not you,
I was me but not me as well,

around the lake for hours like this,
listening to the crush of acorns,
grasping bittersweet from branches,
carrying the tangled strands.

I couldn't look away from everything
losing itself into nakedness
as though old brilliance were unimportant.
This was not a landscape of death,

only heaviness falling from trees.
I remembered how we used to walk
without purpose, as though
we required large terrain,

sometimes never stopping until
the wind pulled back. Renaming
one another in the quiet, bodies
covered in bloom.

Mechanics

My younger son keeps pouring
so the glass remains full:

drinks and laughter around the table
like the old times, the boy times

when they talked to me
about everything—*mechanics,*

in particular: the schemas of
car engines or construction equipment,

the miraculous embroidery
of hard drives, how something

inside a shell could control a world,
be a blueprint, a god, even,

for what we call *the outside.*
Once my younger son

drew the heart
with blue and yellow crayons,

rendering the chambers *extra big*
so there was room for everybody.

There Is No Echo

The doctor tells me I have a small heart
yet it is strong, does not skip,
no reverberation when its doors close.
He holds the strip of paper in his palms
while the nurse removes conductors,
each making a small suckling sound

as it pulls away from my skin.
I joke that my heart is big,
too enormous for most situations
which is why I stand in back
or pay extra for carry-on.
He raises his eyebrows

just a little and says *Nonsense,*
a baby aspirin will help.
I tell him I am certain my heart is frail,
it quakes at scary movies and turns soft
at animals in the road so I have to pull over.
You take this too seriously, he says,

there's always yoga. I assert
that my heart skips all the time,
I feel it thrash against my ribs,
hammer and thwack and jump,
especially on Mondays
when I contemplate what's ahead.

His eyes look dull. *Decaf,* he says.
Finally, I ask him, if there is no echo,
what sound wakes me every night?
I am thinking that the machine
is wrong, the doors of my heart
never close, that is the problem.

Open all the time. Open for business
24/7, customers coming and going.
With a heart like that, there is
a lot of noise. A million returns
and exchanges. *Go have some fun!*
he replies as he leaves. *Live a little!*

Secured Cushions, Beer and Olives

The boat of revelation has whiteness and chrome,
no map or compass; only our thirst

carries us to sea
where the Pacific speaks in tongues,

what you require, what
you call prayer.

People are healed here, people
with crystals on their breasts,

drifting with currents.
Days do not come one after the other

forever, days are not a stretch of water,
days are waves that break.

We sail until the correlates of horizon
release themselves to ocean's open expanse.

Without our locations we do not
need to say, I am here,

you are here, or I am here,
you are not here.

Reading in Calabasas

The medium informs me I was
a nurse in three past lives. *I see you*
applying cotton to wounds with tongs,

she says. *Tongs are for hot dogs,*
I say. Outside the café
the air has grown dense and hot,

pressing against me when the door opens.
I remember one soldier's forgiveness
when I pressed against his wound,

how the stitches wouldn't hold,
the way he whispered
his own last rites.

The medium says I will have more nurse lives
until I accept suffering, that there is no way
to predict it, to stop it.

After the reading I lie down between
cars in the lot, close my eyes
to all the wounds that won't heal,

listen to small acts of hope,
the passersby pausing to ask, *Is she*
hurt, the voices on cells, the sirens.

My Apparition

The afternoon fades against a million
smog-spackled cars that nestle
into underpasses: concrete mutes
the suckle of metal,

the stop-start to our valley,
its sprawl of streets javelined with palms.
My lover, coat in hand, stands in high rise
dusk, watches from his window

the requiem of commuters
play out the day. Waiting for traffic
to die. The ghost of a man hunched
from hours at a screen

merges with reflections from a summer
years ago, miles away.
I have learned to wait, find patience
with patterns of coming and going.

Sometimes it is necessary
to be stuck in traffic.
Everyone overheats, edging
toward a shared destination.

I imagine
he watches a larger apparition.
The amber rivulet below
completes its course,

the western delta
rolls out its darkness,
he stands captivated
by the radiance of us.

Remarkable Winds Come to Our Home

The chimes across the alley
ring all night, a ceramic

mobile our neighbor
made herself. Once

I invited her for tea,
Why on earth, she said.

Nothing between us
but the lonely alley.

In the morning I find
a forest floor of fronds,

branches, new leaves,
so much lost to wind.

My neighbor's chimes
are scattered in shards

on my drive. I pick up
imprints of hearts on

hardened clay. I don't
know whether to return

the fragments. I watch
myself stand at her door,

I am not myself but
a woman in a dream,

doing something ordinary,
stepping beyond old rules.

The wind beginning to
sing against herself.

Not Asking for Much

Of course there were large miracles, the morning
they found seashells in the desert, or the plane ride

through lightning. She misses the smaller ones,
though, images of her mother's hands in the kitchen,

or sounds of her singing. She petitions for them.
What comes is what she doesn't want, what she

prays against: the smells of medicine, of the body
when she bathed it. Changing sheets, watching

the blue stillness of her mother's eyes. Private places
she had to wipe with tissues, sooth with ointments.

How she had grieved for herself, believing no daughter
ought to do such things. How over time the acts became

second-hand, almost beautiful. Almost opportunities,
with their own history, their own faith.

Progeny of a Healer, 130 B.C.

The woman kneels in dirt,
transfigures plants to salves

that relieve suffering;
hangs herbs from rafters

of trees, grinds almonds
with dried petals of summer's rose.

She takes a bite to taste song,
light glazing every sweet creation.

At her hearth a man suffers
for her body, fragrant, muscular;

she blends and heats
all she has gleaned.

The harvest flourishes green,
deep-veined, arching toward light.

Ready for Happiness

Even at rush hour the freeways are lonely.
Everyone and no one. They were on the 110.
Then they were in the lot, the contractions
quickening. *Aren't you ready,* people
were saying. *It looks like it's time.*

A world noticing, its hands on her body.
Walking through automated doors,
not looking back,
grasping her husband's hand
when a woman nearby cried out.

She wanted to turn away from her magnificent
breathing, the sear of muscles bonded
in enterprise, thinking the lights above
were stadium brights. *Don't try to look,*
someone was saying.

But she looked at how simple she was,
stripped of everything but longing.
Around her the people talked about cars
and the upcoming weekend. She knew
they wanted her to keep going.

To hold on, then, when they said, not to
hold on, not to hold back any more.

Signs of Life

At the end of labor,
song was falling
in shafts of heat,
a scorcher one nurse
chanted, the foreign
searing singing,
cleaving the deepness
in me. Something
massive was falling
away, a fortress,
a castle's matrix
of filament
in conflagration.
I blazed above
the red rose
my husband held
until the nick
of stitch, its
rhyme of flame,
my baby's cry
the psalm to
save me.

Talisman

When my children were young
I would pause throughout the day
to be with them in my mind,

thinking to myself *He must be taking a nap,*
or *It's recess, she's playing four-square,*
my way of living through the longing,

of being in my necessary life,
knowing they were in their necessary lives,
even as they missed me. The immensity

of what I chose to do
reconfigured every wall and corner.
I navigated as one who has lost sight.

Some days I felt their need
like my own blood, surging,
every vein inflamed.

I was emptiness but for
their small temples, lit
with a thousand pyrrhic flames.

Biographical Note

Lisa C. Krueger is a poet and psychologist. She is the author of two previous books of poetry, *Rebloom* and *animals the size of dreams*. Her poems have appeared in numerous journals, including *Atlanta Review* and *Prairie Schooner*. She has written a series of interactive journals related to psychology and creativity. She maintains a private therapy practice focused on women's issues, health psychology, writing therapy, and the role of creativity in wellness. She lives in Pasadena, California.